SEASEDGE
publications

PHILLIP SCHOFIELD

FORWARD

How many times have you been whisked back to some childhood memory because of a smell? A strange question to start with, I admit, but it's true isn't it? All of us at some time or another have been spirited away because we caught a brief fragrance of something carried on the wind. The smell of the sea, a hint of perfume, freshly mown grass. These are all common triggers of this most powerful sense. How about acetone? That's mine! Not very romantic and I don't think it would feature very high on many other lists. It's also not the sort of smell you comes across much in the normal scheme of things. However, on those very rare occasions when a trace of acetone finds its way up my nose I am guaranteed a magic carpet ride of childhood memories.

But what on earth is acetone? It's the highly inflammable solvent that cleaned the brushes after they had been used to coat surfboards with polyester resin.

That smell will pick me up and drop me in the Bilbo factory on Pargolla Road Newquay, Cornwall in about … let me see … 1970. I would be about eight and my dad had been working with Doug Wilson for two years or so. He would continue in this line of work for a further ten years.

The factory was such a brilliant place to play, seemingly endless rooms to explore with all manner of machinery to watch and mess with. Firstly there were huge moulds to pour liquid foam into, when it spalshed and dribbled it hardened into wonderful swirling shapes. If I pushed hard enough, I could crunch my fingers right through. If I ever got bored playing with foam, there was always the coloured resin to chip and peel from the walls of the glossing room. All these colours combined in crusty unison on the walls and ran in a unique and one~off modern art tapestry into a multi~coloured puddle on the floor. Then there was Rose. She worked at the factory and always seemed to be smiling. I had to seek her out on my travels because she would give me the next captivating instalment on the little people who lived in the dust extraction system. I never questioned the reason why they would live in such an inhospitable environment because the tales were too good.

The magic portal through which all these memories flow is my dad, the artistic member of the Schofield family. Therefore his talents with surfboard design were to me, second to none. He could easily create a Union Jack, elephant or company logo and was probably the first person ever to spray water colours directly onto a foam blank. Even now I think he quietly swells with pride when he comes across 'one of his boards'.

Surfing in Cornwall has now become a multi-million pound sport, as it has all around the world. Hopefully, soon our local councils and national government will have the presence of mind to invest deeply in this great natural resource. Will they recognise its potential and will that recognition finally encourage them to clean it up and keep it clean? Not just in the short term ~ but for generations of surfers and bathers to come. We don't have to kid ourselves that we have one of the finest stretches of coastline in Europe. That's something to be very proud of ~ but we are kidding ourselves if we believe that it's maintained to an international level of cleanliness and there's nothing but shame to be found in that. Investment in the Cornish coastline has to be money well spent.

It's also important, whether you're about to take the plunge and have a go for the first time or if you're an experienced pro to remember how it all began in this neck of the woods. There's no doubt that it would have started with or without the European Surfing Company, Bill Bailey, Doug Wilson, Freddie Blight, Brian Schofield and all the other major players, because the beaches are too good to waste. There is though, no guarantee that without them your board would have such a fine pedigree.

ABOUT THE AUTHORS'

you should
have been
here
yesterday

4

Rod Holmes is 41, was born on the Wirral and began surfing in the late 1960's in Newquay. He has been a member of the North East-West Surf Club, Croyde Surf Club and Newquay Boardriders and is a past President of the English Surfing Federation. He works as a television journalist and lives in Newquay with his wife Jane and son John.

Doug Wilson, was born in Sussex and first came to Cornwall in 1959 to be a lifeguard. He began his career as a surf photographer in the early 1960's and was one of the pioneers of Britain's surfing industry. He now runs a business in Falmouth and has two children, Carly and Hannah.

F A C E

THANKS

Heritage takes many forms ~ a beautiful building; a piece of music, laced with the fragrance of memory; family history reaching back through times' dark tunnel. Heritage offers a strong human focus ~ a pride in the past and a stake in the future.

This book is about a sporting heritage which has touched the lives of hundreds, influenced the outlook of thousands. When surfing first washed up onto Cornwall's beaches thirty years ago, no~one could predict the hold this mysterious foreigner would have. Britain was about to meet Malibu, Bondi and the Beach Boys head on. What took root was an idealised endless summer of boards, blonde hair, sunshine, girls and travel.

Surfing is as seductive now as it was then. Surfers left school, jobs, homes, wives and girlfriends to be a part of the vibrant new buzz. Doug Wilson was in Cornwall with his camera to record those first barrel~chested pioneers, surfing pristine waves. His images from the early sixties record that faraway place of young dreams, no crowds, golden sunsets, good friends, the shock of cold, clear blue water and the sheer outrageous, electrifying slide across a glass~smooth face of a perfect wave.

Thousands would put their feet in the same footprints on the same beaches as the surfers you see here. Many would do better. Many would do worse.

But none could be what these men were ~ the first. They were 'here yesterday'. The rest of us can only eavesdrop.

I'd like to thank all the people who helped make this book possible and apologise to those who may feel 'they were there' but have been left out. I gratefully acknowledge the help of Doug Wilson for his pictures and memories; John Conway for his recollections and kind and unreserved advice; Roger Mansfield and Chris Jones for their time and effort in relating tales of those early years; my parents, John and Joan, for bringing me to Newquay originally; to Jeff, Pete, Dave and Kevin ~ firsts on other beaches at other times; Graham; Joe & Nance, Dave and Helen and most of all to my wife Jane and son John who know why the town is so special to me. **Rod Holmes, Newquay, Cornwall, 1994**

I would like to thank the late Kam Veeran for introducing me to the surf life-saving association in the late '50's. Also to Dave Taylor and Richard Trewella who were the backbone of the Newquay Surf Life-Saving club when I first arrived in Newquay.
Thanks also to Bill Bailey, Bob Head, Freddie Blight my partners in Bilbo and to Brian Schofield for running the factory. Finally I would like to dedicate this book to my daughters Carly and Hannah
Doug Wilson, Falmouth, Cornwall, 1994

CHAPTER one

"Then ya stand up as quick as ya can...". The addiction begins, summer 1961.

B E G I N

A new swell, a new thrill.
North Fistral, October 1964.

The first of the many
(l to r) Ian Tiley, unknown, Warren Mitchell, Doug Turner, John Campbell, Bill
Bailey, Doug Wilson and Bob Head.
Mawgan Porth, September 1962.

N I N G S

No~one saw them as pioneers. Just a bunch of watermen, idling through another summer. Yet the focus of their fun in the sun was very definitely new. Nineteen~fifty nine was the dawn of surfing in the UK. Newquay Council took on full~time lifeguards at classy beaches from Watergate down to Great Western, Tolcarne and on to the dramatic sweep of Fistral.

Like Australia, surf lifesaving was tops. The clubs (set up a few years before) used single and double wooden surf skis for rescues but had no purpose~built surfboards ~ just their own bodies to swim into and catch waves. Then in 1960, the first long, wooden boards, made of marine ply, found their way into clubhouses up and down Cornwall's north coast.

The skis ~ and these crude, heavy logs ~ were the only way to learn to catch a wave. Short, one~and~a~half meter long plywood planks, surfed lying down and dubbed 'chicken run' boards by older surfers, taught timing and wave know~how. Those lucky enough to have skin diving flippers could swim beyond the breaking set waves and kick into the bigger, green swells. Plenty of fun...but maybe there was more.

That intoxicating magic of stand~up wave riding began two years later. Surfing mushroomed once the boys in the clubs picked up lighter, plastic boards which were revolutionising surfing in the 'States and Australia.

Four Australian lifeguards sauntered down the shaley, pale yellow sands of Great Western one chilly April day in 1962. They pulled their surfer jackets tighter to them against the brisk offshore. No footprints scarred the level tidal wash. Here for the short holiday season, they brought with them nine foot, plastic foam~cored, glass fibre performance boards made in Sydney by Scott Dillon. A three foot set beckoned. They paddled out and ripped every wave apart with a string of turns, cut backs and steep drops. This was a new game ~ of style and strength, power and poise.

Bob Head, Ian Tiley, John Campbell and Warren Mitchell were the innovators. They were Sydney lads ~ mostly from the Avalon Surf Lifesaving Club which had nurtured so many champions ~ who brought walking on water to the Old World.

The Bay in good form.
May, 1964.

Classic longboard style. Jack Lydgate,
Fistral, summer 1963.

Their first jobs were at Watergate with beach owner Ralph Doney. On warm summer nights, Ralph ~ with an eye for pure theatre ~ would send the boys across the Bay to Newquay, towed behind speedboats on their boards, wearing capes and carrying blazing torches. Tolcarne Beach, run by the Daniel brothers, put on evening surfing sessions, drawing big crowds to the mystique of this new sporting spectacle. Once darkness fell, a large, salt~encrusted cave at Great Western made an ideal place for a barbeque. The flames flickered fantastic shapes against the craggy walls and wet, rough roof as surfers huddled with new girlfriends, talking of a rising swell.

Later that spring, expanding the international contingent, came American Jack Lydgate with solid experience from the big waves of Hawaii. By now, local surfers couldn't get enough of these new 'sticks'. Overnight, surfing became a breeze. Plastic boards would turn, trim and paddle so much better than wood because they were lighter. Jack and the boys led the way.

Iron man Trevor Roberts trims into a neat little right at Western in May 1964. Trev's red and black board was his trademark.

Summer arrived. In a shop at the bottom of Marcus Hill, two shorter boards appeared in the window, the first second hand equipment in Newquay. They'd been made in a workshop on Mutley Plain in Plymouth in neighbouring Devon, out of a pair of balsa blanks and then glassed by local waterman Freddie Blight. Freddie had copied shapes he had seen in an American catalogue for sons Richard and Andrew and were probably the first boards of their kind to be made in Britain. A trickle of other boards began turning up from New Zealand, South Africa and America.

When sharing the Bay meant one friend on the same wave. Bill Bailey and Richard Trewella, May 1964.

It was around this time that a clean~cut, car racing, surf~riding band called the Beach Boys were taking surf to the suburbs. Suddenly, every city kid without a wave to his name, tuned into a youth cult which stormed out of the West Coast and rushed around the world. A new era had arrived, 'Flower Power' was just over the horizon and being a surfer meant plugging into a happening of indescribable fun.

Setting up the right. Chris Jones,
Great Western, summer 1964.

Pacific warmth on vinyl was one the ~ the raw Atlantic in the flesh was another. For serious surfers in Britain, though, there was the flip side of 'cool'. No wetsuits placed seasonal limits on surfin' UK unless you were an iron man. You packed up in September and let the board gather dust in the garage rafters until the frosts left with the warmth of spring.

Newquay became the sports' heart in the first two years. Fistral was regarded by many as too dangerous to handle...unless it was summer and the surf was small. Chemists sold cheap bricks of dense, rock~hard paraffin wax which had to be melted over a board's deck to give grip. As cars were scarce, transport meant motor or push bikes.

Early speed line. Watergate, summer 1962.
Sydney's Warren Mitchell angles across a steep left. His board's a ten-six balsa. In spite of the increasing influence of the plastics industry, there were some examples of wooden hulls still around.

The roots of surfing. Fistral,
September 1964.
Like other countries, British wave
riding owed its birth to the surf
lifesaving clubs.
Repeating the experience of
nations all over the Pacific, British
wave riding began life in the
thriving surf lifesaving clubs.

In the hook.
Trev Roberts charges a clean
right during a glassy evening
session at Western,
summer, 1963.

The Australians went a stage further. They'd pick up 'woodies' each year from London on the way west ~ second~hand London taxis were cheap and roomy. These sober black saloons would cruise past drifts of waving seapinks, lining the hot, high summer coast road to Mawgan Porth, boards poking out of the side windows, empty bottles, tins and crushed food under seats and matted carpets.

You could always tell a surfer from his legs ~ large calloused, kneecaps and bumped~up feet, caused by hours of knee~paddling the board out to the lineout, were bloody badges of courage. Boards were still solid and made to last ~ thirty kilos was normal ~ with thick, bottle green resin that fixed two or three stringers and a coveted logo in a chemical aspic. A heavy wooden fin let the board turn gracefully on a sparkling blue face. Surfing was still something to be done with friends, the sun on your back.

Dive and surf. Towan Beach, summer 1963.
Early wetsuits were based on scuba gear. (l to r) Richard Trewella,
Bill Bailey and Brian Daniels.

Remember that early Beach Boys album, with the band holding that blue and yellow square tail? Here,(l to r), Rob Wilson, Roger Mansfield, Colin Christian and Chris Jones parody California style at Great Western.

"When you went surfing", said Chris Jones, a top board maker and sixties surf champion, "you went down the coast in your car and stopped if other surfers came the other way. We'd check each other's boards, find out where we were all heading then join up for a surf. It was very friendly".

The pace quickened. Bob Head started to make boards at Mawgan Porth in 1963 under the label 'Friendly Bear'. On his day, Bob would win most surf lifesaving contests up and down the coast, in a blaze of flags and sunshine. Bill Bailey

shaped in a garage at Porth. Doug Wilson made his living as a surf photographer, printing up postcards for the tourists, as well as running a Newquay surf shop. There seemed to be money in the sport, so with Freddie Blight making up the three surfing musketeers, they launched their own company.

Viv Wilson snags a right at Great Western, summer 1963.

It was a modest yet fateful beginning. The famous Bilbo firm began turning out boards for £25 each in second hand sheds at Pargolla Road in Newquay in February 1965. They marketed the mail order surfing industry as the European Surfing Company and Doug, with a visionary flourish, opened a second shop in Fore Street called the Surf Centre. This professional outfit would turn Newquay into Britain's first surfing mecca.

Life imitates art. First boards amongst the summer crowds.

Great Western, summer 1963. Chris Jones, Viv and Rob Wilson, Roy Heath and Roger Mansfield. Check the competition stripes on boards and deckchairs.

The hands have it.
Emerging style from an
early high performer,
August 1965.

Jack Lydgate picking off
a peak at Fistral.
August 1965.

Surfers travelled from Brighton, Bournemouth, Wales and other parts of the South West to buy new boards, talk, listen and be at the centre of all this energy. Skateboards were also a big draw ~ the rush to get to grips with sidewalk surfing meant Bilbo made and sold their own skateboards for £4 19s 6d~virtually as soon as they came off the bench.

Surfing and pop still went hand~in~hand. Singers like Long John Baldry, Ralph McTell, Donovan, Wizz Jones, Don Partridge and Ian Dury (of 'Blockheads' fame) all came to Newquay. Even Beatle Paul McCartney was seen gazing over Tolcarne, planning, perhaps, a magical mystery surf.

Early local surfing standouts included Chris Jones, Tigger Newling from Treyarnon and Newquay Grammar School boys like Roger Mansfield. All had been influenced by those early Australian travellers. "I watched someone paddle one of the new boards out to sea in 1963, thinking it was some sort of raft and then seeing them riding in standing up. It was a raw and exciting experience, brought to me from another land" said Roger.

Midget Farrelly at Fistral? Almost. It's Aussie Glen Short, September 1966, bringing the style of the world champion to Cornwall.

John Conway, who publishes 'Wavelength' magazine, got his first board in the same year. "It was a second~hand nine~six balsa board made by Freddie Blight, which I bought for £17. I learned the hard way ~ it was so beat up and water logged, when you paddled it, it just sank". John graduated to a board with a de~laminated deck that had also seen better days...it was sheltering weeds in Bill Bailey's back garden but it was the key to a world of delights. He surfed it all that winter with Roger, Viv and Robin Wilson.

The Bay dumped thirty years ago!
Then and now, a large close-out meant a trip to
nowhere. September 1963.

Chris Jones's parents ran the St.Brannocks Hotel above Tolcarne Beach. "My Dad had an arrangement with the lifeguards and deck chair man that they would look after me. Dad would take me to the top of the steps, wave down and I'd stay on the beach all day, playing, watching and listening". Chris rode 'chicken run' boards to begin with, then used flippers to get further outside. At 16, he picked up his first real board, a nine~four Bill Bailey, and joined the other hot teenagers who ate, drank and slept surfing. It was an itch you could scratch with a good afternoon session in a clean four foot swell off Western with four mates...but that divine irriation would be back, nagging as ever, the very next morning.

Take a board, a new ocean and a dash of style...
Bob Head, drop knee turn, summer 1965.

Jack Lydgate races a back-lit curl at
Fistral, summer, 1965.

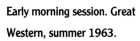

Early morning session. Great
Western, summer 1963.

Baby, light my fire.
Pure theatre from two of the first
group of Australian lifeguards,
setting out for the Bay from
Watergate, summer,1963.

The sport grows. Boards propped
up against the beach wall.
Porthmeor, St.Ives,
September 1965.

There seemed to be plenty of work for older
surfers who wanted it while chasing a life in the
sun. You could survive on ten bob (fifty pence)
a day and still be a dedicated wave follower. The
youngsters had the long school holidays. You
were young. Life was a beach.

Sun or no sun, if the swell was running,
Jack Lydgate would be there.

CHAPTER two

P E

**Dave Friar sweeps off the top at
Tolcarne, July 1967.**
A real stylist, Dave went on to
run his own surf shop in Swansea
and compete at the top level in
UK contests.

Ou est la plage?
Members of an early French surfari.
(l to r). Alan McBride, 'Moby',
Richard Trewella and friends.

O P L E

The word was out. Britain had waves and plenty of them. Viewed by some early travellers as Britain's equivalent of Australia's Gold Coast, Cornwall offered empty line~outs, uncharted snappy beach breaks and classic set~ups, just waiting to be discovered.

Amongst those 1962 pioneers was the tall, powerful Jack Lydgate, as well as Doug MacDonald from San Fransisco. Both men were used to big waves and were mature watermen at a time when most Brits could only stand, stare and fall off. MacDonald surfed in Newquay for a few months then moved on to the warmer weather of Biarritz in France ~ leaving behind his priceless Hobie for the locals to try.

Early travellers outside the old Surf Centre in Newquay, May 1965.

"I swear I just saw Gerry Lopez....."
Tigger Newling (left) and Vince
Ward. Western, June 1969.

Bill Bailey, meanwhile, had moved to Redruth where his parents lived, a town about fifteen miles from Newquay. An early innovator, Bill experimented with blowing his own foam and working with different resins and board shapes. After a few months trials, he developed a reasonable foam blank, the light but rigid plastic core at the heart of every board.

Doug Wilson said "I bought Bob Head's first board and surfed it in the Bay in 1964. By this time, Bill was also shaping and glassing boards, so there was a bit of competition going on, even at that early stage. Surfing ~ then like now ~ was linked to pop music. I was living in Tower Road and someone came round with a little transistor radio with the Beach Boys singing about shooting the curl and Rincon. We'd read about these places ~ but this was the first time we'd heard a pop group making music about them", said Doug Wilson.

Richard Trewella from the lifesaving club and Viv Wilson were amongst those early leaders on malibus. A tall, stocky soldier from the Lifeguards Regiment in London came to Newquay for a holiday ~ and stayed. Trevor Roberts rapidly became one of the best surf lifeguards and his son Grishka would grow up to be a top competitor on the professional European circuit of the 1990s. All watched and learned from the next wave of visiting Australians. Surfers like Brian Campbell and a wildman known simply as Bombhead, made it look so easy. These people ripped with grace and with a fluid aggression in surf from one feet to ten feet.

Checking it out.
Proffesional Rod Sumpter and
company in French woody at La
Barre car park, September 1965.

Stylish Sarah Newling takes a
clean left-hander at Watergate,
September 1967.
In the sixties, girl surfers were rare.
Good girl surfers were even rarer.
Sarah's brothers Tigger and Mike
found fame of their own.

La Barre, summer 1965.
Jim Noll (far left, Greg Noll's brother), Dennis White and
Rod Sumpter with other American and French surfers.

Roger Mansfield said "I was the young gremmie amongst a slowly expanding group of people who hung out on the bottom slope of Great Western beach. Just like the broken down steps in 'Big Wednesday', we had our place, the Slope. To me, surfing in Newquay has its spiritual centre right there. Bill Bailey gave me a chance to have my first go on a board, Trevor Roberts had his deckchair business there and a whole host of fantastic characters, who seemed like older sages, came through those first few years. The peeking order was strong, you knew your place, you felt their power".

Whatever else the surfing life taught, wanderlust was part of the package. Most of these travellers headed south to France ~ as the pictures of an early 'surfari' show when Bilbo decided to spread its commercial net across the English channel. It's fair to say our French neighbours loved it and treated the visitors well.

La Barre's international camp fire,
this time with Charlie Williams, surf
photographer Armand de Rosnay
and other top French surfers.
The French defined style, turning up
at the beach in white Mercedes,
wearing bath robes.

Entente cordial. Outside Bidart town hall, summer 1966.

British and Australian surfers were treated to lunch by French officials after setting up the first local board hire business.

Lunch at Hendaye, summer 1965.
(l to r) Dennis White, Rod Sumpter, unknown, Doug Wilson tuck into petit pain.

Serenade for one.
Doug Wilson (in evening dress) plays 'Last Post' as Bill Bailey leaves the water, Towan Beach, summer 1963. To let surfers at Fistral know he was closing his lifeguard hut each evening, Doug used to blast a few bars on his trumpet!

Not every new~comer was happy to act like a sage. "After one really good surf session at Western", said John Conway, "an Aussie called Chris, who was a real animal, wanted a beer in the Western bar. He had a running battle with the manager who kept banning him for lewd acts. This night, he walked in, asked for a beer but the barman told him to get out.

"Chris promptly walked behind the bar and turned all the beer taps on full. The barman ran behind him, all the way through the pub, turning them off, while Chris just did another lap, turning them all on again. This went on for a few circuits, beer awash everywhere, until Chris said he'd stop if he wasn't barred! Sensibly the barman agreed!"

Power in person.
Rodney Sumpter shoots a full rail wrap up the face of a small Fistral wall. Rodney's early dominance, in contests or in free surfing, was unmistakable. He was born in Britain but grew up at Avalon Beach near Sydney.

A tip classic.
Glen Short going as far
forward as you can. Fistral,
September 1966.

Down in France the following summer, Chris, who had those large, grazed knee bumps, swollen up even larger from a six~hour session at Hossegor, created a minor international incident in Biarritz Post Office. He left a trail of bloody footprints, spattered across the immaculate French floor as he went to buy some stamps!

Early surfaris were underway, some more hand~to~mouth than others. One prominent surfer left Cornwall destined for Portugal. The fact that his woody had no starter motor and a useless first gear didn't seem to matter. His trip almost came to a colourful end ~ while reversing up a hill in France, he opened the door to watch where he was going ~ and promptly fell out! He hauled himself back into the vehicle before it ran too far back down the hill ~ though not before he turned the Biarritz air bluer than the local cheese.

A break in the action.
John Conway, Richard Trewella, Pete Russell, Alan McBride and others at Guethary, October 1966.

New boards ready for the
showroom.
Bilbo craftsmen include Brian
Schofield , Chris Jones
and Dai Jones.

A group of Cornish surfers headed out on the Weymouth ferry for Jersey and a competitive weekend. As soon as they left port, a group of juniors went straight for the bar, boasting about the coming drinking binge now they were away from mum and dad. After two shandies, most of the youngsters were sick over each other, as the ferry pitched up and down in a swell which would make their weekend competition a classic!

The surfing business itself was going through some ups and downs too. Bilbo had shaped two brand new boards for a photo~shoot with some fashion models for 'Petticoat' magazine out at Porth Beach. Doug Wilson put the boards back on top of his van once the session was over ~ but as he drove past the Bristol Hotel on Newquay seafront on the way home, the bungees snapped with the stinging force of two angry bullwhips.

The boards launched themselves skyward like two heat seeking missiles and ended up sliding down the road in a flurry of glass and foam with a series of dull, leaden thuds. Strike four days work in as many seconds. Bill Bailey was not pleased.

"Changing decently to go in and out of the water was always a problem", added John. "We used to nip into the toilets at Western and frighten the little old lady who used to be the toilet cleaner ~ that was after we locked her in one of the cubicles".

Dave Friar, who ran the Swansea
Bilbo Shop, holds another silver-
plated 'scalp'. June 1969.

Chris Jones, Fistral stand-out. Autumn 1963.

Despite the cold, in the years before wetsuits arrived, some surfers managed to stay in the water, winter and summer alike. One such surfer was Dave Patience. 'Moby' was well over six foot tall with a huge beard. He wore nothing but shorts resembling the kit worn by American football stars. Bill Bailey, meanwhile, wouldn't let a little thing like a freezing offshore wind stop him surfing if conditions were right. He'd dip into a bucket he kept in his lifeguard hut and casually tug on four or five soggy tee~shirts to help keep out the cold.

Back in town, eating competitions were some of the rowdiest affairs. Bill, Bob and Trevor would pile into spaghetti Bolognese, curried eggs and ten pints of beer ~ just for starters ~ urged on by friends.

Other talents had emerged by 1966. Dave Friar ~ who went on to manage Bilbo's Swansea outlet ~ Charles and James Williams from St.Ives, Jersey's Gordon Burgis and Steve Harewood, Bobby Maile, Barry Jenkins and North Devon's Tim Heyland all developed strong, personal styles.

Such progression came, in part, from a special source ~ still more Australian visitors. Roger Mansfield again: "Fantastic travellers and surfers like Peter Russell, Johnny McIlroy and Rick Friar had come overland. They were great adventurers who had journeyed the overland route from Australia through India and Afghanistan on motorbikes and had real tales to tell".

Bill Bailey and Doug Wilson on Tolcarne, summer 1963. The blue board was the first foam model made in Britain by Bob Head.

Little Fistral's great shape was a low-tide favourite. Glen Short gets five over, September 1966.

Loading up and heading out.
Bob Head, Rod Sumpter and Dennis White get ready for another European trip from London's Victoria Station, September 1965.

Atlantic meets Pacific.
Doug Wilson (left) with Bruce Brown at Heathrow Airport in 1967. Bruce was in Britain premiering 'The Endless Summer' at a London cinema.

Above all, there was a wonderful sense of brotherhood and cameraderie on the beach and in the water."It was a community of shared activity with so much to learn from those much better than you. Everytime someone from abroad came through from the world where top surfing really took place, we soaked up all we could about what waves were like and what boards surfers were riding", said Roger.

"We were hungry for information when all we had was 'Surfer' magazine once every two months. You never knew what you might discover from every new arrival. Everybody seemed to relate to everybody else and there was a great sense of friendship, both on the beach and in the water. Here was genuine innocence, at a time when there where more beaches than surfers".

To be part of 'the Tribe' was vital. Being identified as a surfer offered its own special pride on the beach.

But surfing mavericks didn't go down well with the establishment. Doug again: "The authorities never liked surfing and did little to promote it. They took a rather dim view of the sport, connecting it with drugs and noise.

"The first skateboard era was universally hated by councils and the police ~ but surfing's popularity was undeniable, drawing tremendous crowds from all over the country for Easter, with brightly painted vans from Liverpool, Glasgow, Manchester, London and Birmingham all lining Fore Street. The Sailor's Arms would be heaving".

"We would be invaded by beatniks one year and hippies the next which in turn brought camera crews and reporters down, looking for sensational stories of sex in the sand. It all got slightly out of hand but we were out of the drab old fifties and into a new wave of pop and surf culture".

There were other ways of getting into the headlines and if the surf went flat, there was still plenty to do. Bill Bailey got hold of an old RAF rescue float (a dinghy for ditched airmen). He fixed some canvass to it and went out sailing in the Bay with a couple of friends. Disaster struck on a capsize when the float sunk.... releasing a huge patch of green dye for aerial recognition into the water. Bill and crew were bobbing up and down in the dye ~ and when Bill clambered ashore once the inshore lifeboat towed them in, he was tinted green from head to foot.

Inevitably, a move to warmer shores was on the cards quite early for some Newquay locals. Brian Colwill went to Australia in 1967. Nicknamed 'The Chin' because of a prominent lower jaw, Brian would often volunteer to play the part of a drowning swimmer for life~savers off Great Western Beach, bobbing around in the line~out, waiting for someone to rescue him. Brian's now a lecturer in Brisbane.

Hey there, Georgie Girl!
'Petticoat' magazine photo-shoot at
Porth Beach, summer 1966.

Dennis White from Sydney bottom turns into a strong, overhead left at La Barre, summer 1965. This famed French big wave break was virtually destroyed three years later by coastal 'improvements'.

a neat cocktail cabinet, complete with delicate miniatures. Bill Bailey's Ford van even boasted a complete single bed in the back.

When mini~gun and stubby vee~bottomed tracker shortboards arrived in during the late sixties, surfing became faster and totally radical. Boards dropped in length to seven and eight feet. Most adapted well to this brash, new equatic revolution ~ especially youngsters, who found the heavy nine~footers almost impossible to turn and trim.

"The lifestyle of the beaches attracted a certain type of person. Surfing was for those who didn't get a kick out of an ordinary existence. Sun and surf was always a strong combination. It still is", said Doug.

That 'strong combination' appealed to characters who relied on their wits for survival and a quirky sense of style. Jack Lydgate, for instance, ran an ancient VW van that contained

"As boards got shorter, good surfers like Chris Jones adapted and refined their style. Surfing became faster and more energetic after the leisurely pace of the longboards" said Doug. The guard changed. Nigel Semmens and Graham Nile moved up through the ranks in competition and free surfing. Martin Geary turned up in 1966 and began making innovative boards; Mick Jackman ~ whose brother Dave was one of the first to ride huge waves in Australia ~ set up the successful Maui Surf Shop opposite Bilbo.

Psychedelic hearse. Jersey car park, 1969.

At first, it had been possible to recognise every new board made by Bilbo and virtually every surfer in Europe. Gradually, the pace quickened and the easy~going stroll of those early years gave way to a beach life in the fast lane. New voices on the 'phone, new faces in between sets, new problems in dealing with fewer waves and more surfers.

Every country in Europe with a beautiful stretch of coastline that had surf, began to feel the pressures. In France for instance, Peter Viertel ~ regarded by many as the father of French surfing and husband of actress Deborah Kerr ~ witnessed a great surge in popularity, as more surfers tried to escape the building crowds on the Cote de Basque. France, of course, had her own heroes ~ Joel and Armand de Rosnay, Michelle Barland, Jo Moraiz, Jean~Marie and Francois Lartigau, Marie~Christine and Marc Delanne.

Many in Britain and abroad felt surfing and crowds would nerver mix ~ but there was no stopping the giant wave of popularity which pushed surfing's dawn into a bright new day.

Bay watch.

Jack Lydgate in his lifeguard chair, August 1966.

C O N T

NUT
480

CHAPTER three

Waiting for a winner.
Spectators watch the GB Nationals
at Watergate, June, 1969.

From the first wave of the judges starting flag, the early contest scene became a celebration of the best the sport could offer. More than just a weekend battle for a trophy, major contests like the Cornish Open or British Nationals provided a festive, focal point for surfers all over Britain.

Originally starting out as short, knock~about sessions between friends keen, to see who was best on a Sunday afternoon, they rapidly developed into two and three day events, usually over Bank Holiday weekends, taking advantage of warmer waters and the sunny seasons of spring, summer and autumn.

Everything became better organised and more sophisticated. Promotors soon realised they had a sporting 'ace' up their sleeves~ the natural drama of semi and final heats which offered Sunday or Monday afternoon highlights to draw the crowds. Heat organisation, too, became more subtle, with heat sheets, experienced judges, accurate timing and air horns to replace frantic waving. The idea was to imitate events a world away in America, Hawaii or Australia.

Tribes gathered on Friday night. VW buses, splotched in gaudy flowers and crowned with rusting roof racks, stacked high with boards, would rattle into Newquay, Bude, St.Ives, Perranporth or Porthtowan. The Beatles, The Move, the Beach Boys and dozens of other pop sounds would blare out from cosy bus interiors. The first beach fires roared into life with the

setting sun. You'd met friends from Wales and London, Liverpool and Aberdeen, swopping tales and jokes of 'the last surf trip', who's travelling, new board shapes, girls, tales of 'bum sessions' and classic conditions.

Contest day! Up early, taking drops on clean swells with the rising tide and hopes for an easy draw. Flags, crowds, judges, wins, defeats went past in a montage of summer sights and sounds. Floaters and aerials were unheard of ~ unless they were unintentional and led to spectacular wipe~outs. Surf leashes were for the future ~ if you lost your board, you swam.

Roller-coasting off the top of some
small but co-operative Fistral wash.
This is August 1969 and the
Australian influence of eight feet,
stubby 'vee' bottomed boards, with
'animal' involvement was knocking
nose-riding into the back seat.

E   S   T   S

The heat is on.
Competitors in the Jersey Gold Leaf
event line up for the quarters,
August 1965. Bob Head works out
his strategy.

The British Surfing Association got going in the mid~sixties and gave a formal stamp to the staging of amateur contests. Sponsorship was never too far away for the handful of professional events. Players Gold Leaf cigarettes, for example, provided the cash for a big Jersey event at St.Ouen's in 1965 ~ apparent contradictions about sport and smoking still hadn't been settled. It was a well run, prestigious event.

"The National Contest emerged as a big event early on, but at first most competitions were small and low~key", said Roger Mansfield. "The first and most memorable contest was the Cornish championships held at Porthtowan, when people would gather from different areas to enjoy surfing".

"No~one really thought you could make big money out of contests but they were an important part of the scene. They were always well attended with some events attracting tens of thousands of people. For most, the whole reason for entering was just to have a good time and let surfers pit themselves against their contemporaries. Judging wasn't too technical ~ it was just a matter of who got the best rides", said Doug.

By now, areas other than Cornwall had their share of good contestants. In South Wales, for instance, Howard Davies, Robin Hansen, Roger Bateman, Viv Ganz, Dai Williams and Adrian Husbands all attracted local respect.

"St.Ives was very much the other centre of surfing identity south of Newquay. It was really only the other large 'town' of surfers and probably had a bigger surfing community then than it does now", said Roger.

Not all of the early events were as mannered as memory allows. John Conway again: "Some contests could be really aggressive. At one event in St.Ives, I got through a couple of rounds, then got drawn with a couple of Jersey guys who were determined to get first and second. One guy blocked me and as I was paddling out, one ran straight over me, put a ding in my board about six inches long and slashed my wrist. It was pretty relentless".

Knee~paddle take~offs, hang~fives, hang~ten, quasimodos, Standing Island Pull~Outs, roller~coasters, 'stink~bug' squats and walking~the~board footwork were what the judges wanted to see. The Bilbo team ~ and many others ~ pulled them off with ease. At one stage, the Company had a huge stack of trophies lined up on shelves in the Pargolla Road factory, all won by its team riders.

Gallic style means a more relaxed stroll to the water's edge for these contestants. France, September 1965. Nearest the camera, Aussie Dennis White.

They're off!

Sprint beach start for the twelve surfers in the Cornish Open at Porthtowan, summer 1966.

National newspapers would come down for contests to dip their big toes in the Atlantic to see what all the fuss was about. The Sunday Times, Express, Mail, Daily Sketch all sent reporters and photographers to follow events and write pieces about the new craze. Features on the new sport even turned up in such unlikely places in 1966 as the Jaguar Owners Handbook!

One reporter wrote "There's many a board rider who thinks that Britain is a wipe~out for surf. But Cornwall has its moments...in Newquay they have the man's answer to a girl's mini~skirt ~ maxi~shorts for protection against chafed legs. A wave of bright beach gear has washed into Britain".

Another watched Australian Rod Sumpter at work, winning everything in sight. In 1967, Rodney Sumpter was the clear favourite to win the Open title at the Nationals. Rodney, the reporter noted, tended to stay apart from the rest of the crowd and away from the beach when he wasn't surfing in a heat. Being a professional meant not getting drunk at local pubs, not making a great play of waxing his board in front of the teeny boppers.

Rodney was pointing the way towards a new professionalism, an insistance that surfing could be much more than a weekend diversion. He wasn't too impressed with the hippie side of hip ~ just a belief in the future of a sport which could earn him a living, dominated by fast, functional surfing in the most critical part of the wave. Rodney was bringing a single~mindedness which pre~dated the rich, professional world tour of the nineteen~eighties. He wanted to win in those early days of contests. His drive meant that he usually did.

The sports commercial base still had a long way to go. "Things were pretty casual. Perhaps there would be a scaffolding stand on the beach but other than that, there were no trade tents. We were still at the stage were there were few hassles on the beach over winning and losing. Contestants just accepted things, especially when they were drawn against Rod", said Doug.

Judges check tide and swell conditions.
Watergate, September 1969.

"There would only be a couple of dozen entries to make up the contest, sometimes with only one division. At some events, there wasn't even a category for women ~ Sarah Newling and Gwyneth Haslop just joined in with the men".

The shortboards which gripped the surfing world by the throat in 1969 caused some confusion amongst judges. Surfers didn't quite know what to make of this new slashing style, with an emphasis on 'involvement'. Quick direction changes and a move to use the wave's vertical face became the norm. But everything settled down and a more dynamic, driving phase in surfing's development hammered the final nail into the coffin of the School of Cruise. Many felt it wasn't for the better. Others were impressed by surfing's new vigour, new energy.

Chris Jones witnessed this shock of the new. "I was surfing on Great Western one night. This fellow walked down the beach, changed into his wetsuit, had a really nice board at about eight foot which was quite short for that period. He paddled out and just shredded. It turned out it was Australian champion Keith Paull, who could do these fantastic paddle out take~offs. He watched a curl coming towards him on the way out, pushed the front of the board into the face, stood up and dropped in".

45

Off-the-top and into the finals.
Tigger Newling launches himself into
a berth in the last round. English
Nationals, August 1969.

The eight feet long, wide~backed 'vee' bottoms from Australia ~ some with fins seventeen inches long , were changing the way people approached the sport, both on the beach and in the water. Things would never be quite the same again for Britain's first generation of surfers.

 "Whether it was contests or free surfing, the way you surfed was changing alot. You could hang down a wave, flop the board onto one flat of the 'vee' and the board would charge round corners at huge speeds; back onto the other 'vee' and scream back down the face. They never lost any speed through turns", said Chris.

Crowds at the GB contest, September 1969.

Chris Jones adds another win to his string of victories.

To the victors, the spoils.
Reg Prytherch, BSA Chairman
(centre), presents top honours to
Jersey's Gordon Burgis. GB contest,
September 1969. Dave Grimshaw
with his back to the camera.

Popular local wins.
North Coast locals Roger Mansfield,
Chris Jones and Alan MacBride step
up to the winner's rostrum.

Focused attention.
The essence of competition, in or out
of the heat sheets. A clean right,
hands and arms predicting a speed
line out of a hooking curl - thirty
years before the ASP. Jersey's Steve
Harewood puts it all together

Solid stance for a backside trip to the semis.
Jim Noll, Greg's brother, at a Guethary event in the summer of 1965.

The amateur contests of the early and mid 1960's were the forerunners of big professional events of the mid and late 1980's. In some respects, the intrinsic elements that made contests so engaging have never changed. True, there was a strong movement away from competition in the 1970's when many surfing centres went 'underground' as a new fashion rejected competitiveness.

But the spice of a weekend in the water, matching yourself against a club or a friend down at the next break, in a bid to come out tops (either for a humble silver~plated trophy or forty thousand dollars) proved just too seductive. It could be serious fun...but fun nevertheless.

The Tigger Newlings, Graham Niles and Rod Sumpters, were, in some respects, the spiritual forefathers of the Martin Potters, Tom Currens and Sunny Garcias. They might easily shake hands across the years ~ and be as equals.

Bottom turning into a small face racks up the points.
Dennis White again.

Waiting for the results.

Alan McBride and Vince Ward. June 1969.

CHAPTER four

The company van sets out with another shipment of boards, late sixties.

T H E
i n d u

Can I help you? Bilbo stand,
Earls Court, summer 1966.
Completely sold out of leashes,
rash vests, deck grip, videos,
wetsuits and thrusters! Just have
to make do with a nine~six for
£25, a Greg Noll poster at 8/~,
'This Surfing Life' at 39/6d and a
copy of 'Surfer' for 5/6.

stry

A new era, a new direction. Pargolla Road Bilbo factory under construction, late sixties.

Pocket rockets,

summer 1969.

In the autumn of 1964, Bob Head and Bill Bailey got in touch with Doug Wilson with the idea ~ as we've seen ~ of setting up a business. Freddie Blight was to be the financial director of the European Surfing Company. The partners bought a plot of land down at Pargolla Road in Newquay (which also had some sheds) and started work in February 1965.

Doug lead the way with the first surf shop in the town ~ possibly in Europe ~ around The Whim area in 1963. "I stocked it with a few odd bits of surfing gear that I managed to scrounge, plus some shorts which I was having made down in St Ives out of heavy sailcloth, selling for £4.19s.6d. It was pretty hand~to~mouth but it was a start."

A second shop soon followed. The Surf Centre opened in Fore Street in the spring of 1965 as business boomed. Once Pargolla Road showed a profit, the businesses combined into one melting pot.

'Porky' Morcom getting in some

research and development,

June 1965.

Just like the sport, the surf industry attracted a rich and varied range of real 'characters', who brought fresh skills and new ideas to the business. Andy Pickles and 'Porky' Morcom, for example, were regular hands in the shaping and glassing rooms.

"We had an influx of overseas surfers coming in. People like Bob Cooper from America, 'Wheels' Williams and Keith Paull, both from Australia. The big event, though, was the arrival of Rod Sumpter, with his ideas from around the world", said Doug.

Competition for the growing market was forever snapping at Bilbo's heels. By the mid 1960's, Freddie Bickers in Newquay, Keith Slocombe in St.Ives, Bob Groves in Bournemouth and Tim Heyland with Tiki in North Devon all had an increasing regional and national following. A whole host of small 'garden shed' producers set up shop, catering for friends, trying out new shapes and production techniques. Boards were still averaging out around nine feet in length, following nose~rider, step~deck and egg~railed trends set in California and Queensland.

The Surf Centre with some Aussie customers.

Either that or the boys were after some Chippendale furniture to ride! May, 1966.

Almost ready. The new Bilbo premises take shape.

John Conway ~ who opened his own board company in the summer of 1970 ~ began his career in 1964 with Bickers. He had served his apprenticeship as a cabinet~maker. "Freddie Bickers opened at the back of St.Thomas' Road in Newquay around the time my Dad was shopfitting Bilbo. Dave Friar left Bilbo and came over to us and Brian Schofield, Phillip Schofield's Dad, joined us too. Later, the Australian Mick Jackman became a shaper. We were only a small concern, turning out three boards a week.

"Like any sixteen year old, I did all the crappy jobs like sanding, glossing, laminating and pin~lines. But I soon moved up. Brian left to join Bilbo, we had a shipment of 20 blanks of new Clark foam from America and Fred said I might as well work the winter out making hire boards for the coming season. Fred virtually gave me the run of the place for six months, shaping, laminating, glassing, the whole deal. Chris Jones worked with me before he went to Bilbo, so as a couple of teenagers, we had our own surfboard factory. It was a dream come true".

Bilbo, meanwhile, realised they needed a bigger, permanent factory in place of the wooden sheds, to keep up with the demand for boards. Dust extraction plant and central heating made the new premises THE most up~to~date board factory.

"It was a fabulous set~up", said Chris Jones, who was a shaper there. "It was probably the best purpose~built factory ever in Europe, turning out 40 boards a week. That rose to nearly 60 when Pete 'Mooney' McCallum joined us. We put out basic 'mals' at first, then dropped to mini guns and shorter boards". Another shaper joined the team. He was Paul Holmes ~ future editor of 'Surf Insight', Australia's 'Tracks' and America's 'Surfer' magazine.

Flower power.
New logo, reflecting the naturalised flow of peace and love.
Summer 1969.

PHOTO: DOUG WILSON

BOB HEAD, NEWQUAY

BILBO SURFBOARDS　　　**EUROPEAN SURFING**
COMPANY LIMITED

EUROPEAN SURFING CO. LTD . BRITISH SURFING CENTRE, PARGOLLA ROAD, NEWQUAY, CORNWALL. TELEPHONE NEWQUAY 4501
CUSTOM BUILT BOARDS TO YOUR OWN SPECIFICATIONS. THE FINEST SURFBOARDS IN EUROPE

Business was in full swing. A new custom board would set you back £25 in 1965, a pop~out a little cheaper. Despite the toughness of a select group of hardmen, wetsuits in Britain were a must. By 1966, Doug was importing O'Neill suits from California, followed by 'home grown' products from Typhoon, who set up a factory in Liskeard in Cornwall. Dennis Cross at GUL was another innovator. The price tag for his product ~ just £15.

"When I first met Dennis", said Doug, "he was cutting out Britain's first wetsuits from the back of a van at Fistral Beach. British rubber was much heavier than American or Japanese material and his first suits were largely just a vest or shortie style to keep out summer chills".

Chris Jones, like many others, made his first wetsuit. "You went down to Central Sports, ordered your double skin, unlined, three~sixteeths neoprene, borrowed a pattern off somebody, drew onto the rubber, cut it out, stuck it together and taped it.

"They were extremely warm suits but every time you took them off, you ripped out a flap or something. You'd take them off and your body would actually steam in cold weather!"

Bilbo started to make skateboards in 1965 after first importing Roller Derby models from the USA. Using Hobie wheels and complete Hamaco units, the Company's mail order business soared.

Board customers, meanwhile, were demanding higher standards as the magazines and films brought the flavour and quality of surfing's centres of excellence to British beaches. Surfers wanted immaculate, dirt~free finishes, sophisticated artwork, deck patches, double rail overlaps and lighter, high performance blanks. A work of art, in fact, as much as a functional board.

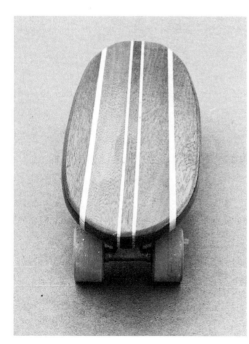

Skateboard equivalent of Hawaiian koa wood board, 1965.
No urethane, no kicks, no Skate Rags, no ramps, no sealed bearings. Wheels by Hobie, deck by Bilbo. This is thought to be the first commercial skateboard in Europe.

As surfers became more aware of the benefits of fine~tuned equipment, technical advances kept pace with the spirit of 'involvement'. Magazine ad, 1968.

Doug said "We used to blow all our own blanks but the foam wasn't that light. We tried to improve them ~ we even went to see a British Aircraft Establishment scientist at Farnborough to see about using carbon fibre to strengthen the glass ~ but eventually we had to import American Walker blanks because their cell structure was much denser and lighter. Bennett foam from Australia was coming in which was also a great improvement.

There was a tremendous upheaval, largely because of what surfers could see in 'Surfer' magazine. Shapes changed every month and you had to keep pace with what surfers wanted. We could produce 30 or 40 boards a week at a stretch and over the winter of 1967, stockpiled almost 500 boards, ready for the rush which we knew would come once the weather warmed up".

Then as now, the magnetism of a board factory would draw surf~hungry gremmies.

"I used to love hanging round companies like Bilbo", said Roger Mansfield, "sweeping up the factory's shaping room, tidying up for a bit of money, or to get free surfboards. By now, I had started to do well and had joined Bilbo's surfing team". Roger won the Cornish junior crown in 1965 and would go on take a string of senior and European titles.

"My problem was that Chris Jones, who was three years older, would always beat me. I'd always come second, so I had to wait for him to move out of the way into the seniors before I could claim my own".

Pride of place. That Bilbo stand at Earls Court Boat Show. London 1967.

Magazine ad, 1968

Board shops had a certain delicious magic, entrancing surfers who would be happy to just stand and stare. It was something you HAD to be part of ~ to soak up the atmosphere. It was all so new, the sights, sounds and smells of an exotic way of life, using new materials with strange, spacey properties.

"The sport had never really been seen before, only a handful of people did it and it was sophisticated because it used glassfibre and foams which gave us something incredibly esoteric. To hang around the shop was to get an education, where you met other surfers, where you learned more of the craft, more about the whole art of surfing", said Roger.

The onset of those shortboards ~ when two and three feet were chopped off the length of early era malibus ~ brought equipment and technological changes that created new headaches for the board makers. Single fins disappeared almost overnight in place of smaller twin~fins, some of which were detachable using polycarbonate 'boxes'. Bob Head developed the 'tunnel' fin which was a glassfibre semicircle, foiled and placed precisely near the tail, predating designs of the 1980's.

Boards outside Bilbo's primitive surf factory, May, 1966, prior to a major rebuild.
The film crew were down from London to make a news item about the popular new sport.

John Conway was part of that progressive second wave of board makers in Newquay. "After we came back from Morocco over the winter of 1969, I decided to start my own company. My Dad had a friend who was a saw sharpener with a spare workshop behind the back of the Belmont Club, so I took that over to make my own boards. The first year, Pete 'Mooney' McCallum came to work with me as a shaper while I finished the boards off. After that, John Hall, another Australian, joined me for two years before he went on to Tiki. I used to employ other guys from Australia who were excellent shapers who would do a couple of dozen boards then move on".

John did well. He had a hard~core base of one hundred customers, keen to support a progressive outfit, selling out of Mick Jackman's Maui Shop, where John had previously worked evening shifts in the summer.

"I actually made Mick's first board sale. We'd built a Bickers board to use as a counter, as a sort of gimmick. It was ten~foot~six long, bright red and highly polished, really beautiful. A guy walked in one night before we had a chance to set it up and bought it straight off' said John.

Up to then, Mick's shop had been retailing Platt's surf shorts, Australian baggies of some quality, designed by Jean Platt over in Oz. "It was incredible", said John, "it was the first custom surf shorts shop with pattern books where you could walk in, get measured up and three days later, you had the best pair of shorts on the beach".

What the best dressed surfer wore in 1966.

Note Vince Ward's knee and foot callouses.

The end of an era. Bilbo factory fire aftermath, September 1970.

The shops would attract both valued customers ~ and those who occasionally turned up with a price on their heads. In the sixties, drugs were rife and at one stage, Doug said Bilbo was drawn unwittingly into an abortive 'bust'.

"Visiting surfers would turn up at the shop, backpacking, on the look~out for work. One chap left his pack in the shop while he looked for somewhere to stay ~ but someone must have tipped off the police that our visitor had cannabis and that he was hiding it in Bilbo. I was serving one evening, watching out for any shoplifters from the stairs, when a chap came in the front door, another through the back and served me with a search warrant.

Old Bilbos never die.
What ever happens to those countless thousands of boards which end up as backyard junk? Foam and resin aren't bio~degradable. Cast~offs, September 1970.

"They kicked all the customers out, kept all the staff in, searched through my van, all the stock and frisked me. It was ironic really because I must have been the only person in Britain who wasn't smoking pot! They found nothing. Simply apologised and left".

Little by little, costs crept up. An increasing amount of money from sales of clothing, jewellery and other surf industry products went to support the expensive board~making side of the business. Companies struggled under higher wage bills and a staggering 25% purchase tax. One by one, the original pioneers of that first flourish of the surfing industry diversified, were absorbed into other firms or simply vanished. And volitile chemicals created their own hazards. In the autumn of 1970, a disasterous fire wrecked the Pargolla Road plant.

As time passed, other highly~regarded and successful firms came and went, imported boards with prestigious names arrived in mysterious packing crates and the clothing industry became a world~wide, multi~million dollar operation, dominated by big names like

Quiksilver, Ocean Pacific, Hang Ten, Rip Curl, Lightning Bolt, Gotcha and Billabong.

For Newquay, the legacy of the sixties ~ and its place as a European surfing capital ~ remains. Doug Wilson believes it's that timeless, random combination of situation and circumstance.

"Newquay's beaches have always been so good, it was a busy tourist town and surfing came in at the precise moment when the youth cult exploded all over the world. It was natural to make it a mecca for the sport. The reasons why it was the right place then, still make it the right place now".

Another satisfied customer. New board, first session, May 1968.

With club patches and sponsors' logos on his baggies, Rod stalls into a
beachbreak left during the Cornish Open, summer 1965.
His fierce competitiveness and sheer professionalism was fifteen years
ahead of the pack in Europe.

CHAPTER five

The Man

'The Man' in poker terms, is the high roller who never loses; the consumate stylist with tricks up his sleeve; the performer with a sharp sense of survival, drawing from a bagful of experience; the craftsman in control any situation. For surfing in Britain in the mid sixties, Rodney Sumpter was 'The Man'.

Rodney burst onto the European scene from Avalon Beach near Sydney, a dark~skinned, gangly, open~faced teenager, with a white hot style. He'd had a starring role in Bruce Brown's "Endless Summer". He was the 1963 Australian Junior Champion who had also won the US Junior Championships at Huntington Beach in California and had surfed Hawaii's North Shore on a promotional visit with the WindanSea Club.

Rod had already blitzed his way through top European competition in Jersey in 1965 and was now set to take mainland Britain by storm. British summertime water wasn't much colder than the Pacific in winter ~ and Rodney was amazed by the number and variety of beaches the Old Country had to offer, whether it was in Cornwall, Devon, Wales, Scotland, or the North Sea. He simply mesmerised Britain with his total command of a surfboard.

Rod was born on 27th May 1947 near Watford, London but had emigrated with his parents to Australia when he was nearly five. He'd longed to see his birthplace and as a successful teenager, fresh from the USA, he checked out Britain's potential. Although Rod returned fleetingly to Australia to visit his parents, he had made up his mind to adopt the UK. On 6th May 1966, he got on a plane at Sydney bound for Britain ~ and Britain got her first true surfing professional.

**Sumpter sets up for five over at
Fistral, 1965.**

"It was a big event when Rod arrived", said Doug. "He was the best surfer we had ever seen. Because of his sporting reputation, he was put on a pedestal by local surfers. He came to our factory and put forward lots of ideas about board shapes and the latest techniques from the States and from Sydney. He was a major contributor to board improvement in Britain. He would ride for Bilbo, we would give him boards, promote him and pay him to shape signature models".

This partnership helped both surfer and Company. It also gave birth to one of the strongest and most memorable images of a new~found personal and national pride in the sport. When Rodney joined the British team for the World Contest in the late sixties, he chose a huge Union flag to cover the deck and bottom of his board. It became his trademark, and everyone wanted the Flag on his Britannia signature model.

"He was high spirited and had a lot of drive to promote his own abilities within the sport. Rod was so hot, he'd give exhibitions of surfing at Watergate and Tolcarne. His technique was quite phenominal".

"At the time", said John Conway, "Rod was virtually Junior World Champion, having won in Australia and California. The first time I saw him surf made me realise he was special. Before he arrived, Paul Kemnitzer from California was the guy all us kids wanted to copy ~ but Rodney was a completely packaged, professional surfer with nose~riding, sponsorship, the lot. Doug Wilson had been importing surf movies and Sumpter's style was as good if not better than most of the Americans we saw on the silver screen because he was more aggressive.

Back arched, effortless stance, perfect trim.
Rod at Fistral, 1965.

Wake surfing on the Camel
Estuary at Padstow.
June 1965.

The Man at work.
Rodney set the pace, whether he
surfed in a contest or in a free
session. Fistral, September 1966.

On a promotional tour of France with Bilbo, September 1965.
The other two surfers are (left) Frenchman Joel de Rosnay
and Aussie 'Wheels' Williams.

"Rod was pulling off snappy manoeuvres while the Americans were all flowing nicely. Even when Rodney first went onto a shortboard he was still better than anyone over here. Rodney had the right attitude. He had a belief that he could win anything and would go out in any surf, small or large, and treat it like a heat in a competition. Every wave would be ridden to the beach with lots of style and finesse. Other guys would say the surf was crappy and wouldn't bother but Rod would be out there".

Such professionalism steamrollered lesser athletes when the competition heat sheets were posted. If you happened to draw The Man in an early round, your hopes at a shot at the final were pretty much over before they began.

"Sumpter was already high up in the competitive stakes", said Chris Jones, "and he brought new ideas about boards into town. Everybody used to have these reverse fins on their boards which were made out of wood and looked like big dinner plates. He brought in the idea of the Sumpter cut~away skeg which was more like a dolphin's fin and surfed wonderfully".

Rod linked his sport with cine~photography, recording the first film images of British surfing to show at local halls all over Europe. Those early efforts with girlfriend Simonne Renvoize included "With Surfing In Mind" and "Come Surf With Me". They contained classic images of those early, empty summer waves, coupling them in a double bill with top~notch American and Australian surf movies like "A Life in the Sun" and "Evolution".

'Gopher' was so good, the European Surfing Company went on a promotional tour to Biarritz in the autumn of 1965, along with Doug, Bob Head and another Aussie surfer called Dennis White.

Easy does it. Rod stays on board in the shallows. September 1967.

Flying the flag. Sumpter trims into a small, hollow inside section at the GB Championships at Fistral, September 1967. The Union flag design of his Britannia model was his trademark.

"Once he got on that board, he was marvellous, in a class of his own. He was both fluid and aggressive at the same time, with a smooth, elegant, functional style which seemed right for every kind of surf. You would never see that sort of riding now because thrusters dictate a different style. Rodney was so hot, people would come from all over to watch when he was in competition. He was simply outstanding, world class. A lot of people tried to copy him ~ but there was only one Rodney", said Doug.

Rodney certainly had it all. He could walk the board with sure and certain moves, produce a cat~like arch in fast, steep sections of the wave, effortlessly trim for maximum speed, head~dip and tuck into tubing sections without getting his hair wet and then pull~out with a swift and graceful sweep.

The impact of Sumpter as that integrated professional lasted throughout the sixties and well into the seventies. He competed for Britain at the San Diego world contest in 1966 (when he came fifth, beating top Aussie Midget Farrelly); at Puerto Rico in 1968, both as part of the Irish team and as an independent surfer; and for Britain again at the Bells~Joanna event in 1970. In every contest, he drew praise and respect.

Rod took the switch to shortboards in his stride and beat younger surfers on the new equipment for some years after surfings 'Big Bang' of 1968, when board lengths dropped dramatically. The Man still showed the surfing world what it meant to be that determined professional who heard a different drummer.

Rodney tackles a rivermouth section near La Barre, November 1966.

Nobody did it better.

Sumpter's cat~like grace and stylish simplicity made him Britain's hottest surfing property in the early sixties.

**Checking out La Barre.
The group includes Bob Head
and Dennis White.**

He would spend some years away from the sport in the 1970's and 80's. But Rod made a remarkable comeback in his forties to qualify for the amateur British team in the longboard event for the world contest in Japan in 1990. Fittingly, his old friend and former world champion, Nat Young, started his second rise to fame at the same time during what became a longboard revival which continues to this day.

Although Rodney was disappointed with his Japanese performance, after narrowly going out in the early rounds, his dedication and effort to return to mainstream competition stood as a fine example in a sport which demands persistence and grit.

Doug Wilson has the last word. "Rod was the man of the moment. He could be difficult, he could be enormous fun and a good friend, with huge reserves of optimism and an outlook on life that said anything was possible. I'm not sure you'd find anyone like him again".

Sumpter takes the Open title at the British.
Watergate, September 1969.

CHAPTER six

How Big?
The crowd gathers on Towan Head for the big swell of 1966. Check the rising wall behind the second line of white water.

BIG WAVES

Older surfers tell tales of days when swells seemed bigger, lasted longer and had a classic, never~to~be~repeated quality. We all do it, sooner or later. No matter where you live, every surf beach has its day, a time when the variables of wind, tide and swell combine to offer an all~time session. It's a day when the usual wave indicators make no sense; when giant sets shake the cliff top; when take off and paddle out points are nothing like the regular set up; when the horizon lifts like the end of the world; when only a handful are ready and willing to meet the challenge.

"Surfers like Roger Mansfield, Trevor Roberts, Chris Jones and the Jersey boys never turned down an opportunity to surf big waves. By far the biggest in the early days was The Cribbar", said Doug.

The Cribbar ~ along with a handful of other big British breaks like Porthleven and Thurso ~ would boil and line~up on only a few occasions each year. The gnarled jagged reef lies off Towan Head to the north end of Fistral. On strong south and westerly swells, with the sun out and a light offshore, the paddle~out channel from Little Fistral looks makeable, almost inviting. But looks can be deceiving.

Set waves march in from almost half a mile out. Sets of three, pitching at fifteen feet at four minute intervals are common. Some of Newquay's older and well respected surfers claim Cribbar doesn't work as well or as often as it used to, largely because of the huge quantities of sand, which have been moved around by winter storms over the past two decades, changing the bottom profile. Others say it still gets good.

"Thirty years ago, Cribbar always looked to be breaking better because maybe we didn't know a lot about big waves. Perhaps it looked to be a better wave than it does today because people had limited experience", said John Conway. "Fishermen in Newquay reckon that back in the 1940's, the coast used to get more

History in the making.
Two~shot sequence of a surfer ~ thought to be Johnny McIlroy ~ on a
giant left which ran around Towan Head, heading for the Mystic Rock.

south~westerly swells with south~easterly winds and they used to have to sail a quarter~of~a~mile around Cribbar because it was so big".

John remembers fishing off the Fly Cellars as a child and watching the local lifeboat bringing the remains of large yachts into harbour which had been pounded to matchwood off Cribbar. Three people had drowned.

"Cribbar always used attract the surfers who really knew what they were about. Bob Head and Jack Lydgate were stand~outs, Jack being a big wave rider from Hawaii who knew about massive surf. The peaks seem to have changed out there. I don't recall seeing it work exactly like it used to. The reef went through a period in the mid~sixties of really coming on, throwing up mountainous conditions. But there doesn't seem to be as much interest in riding it now".

Chris Jones added "I remember trying to paddle out one day from Little Fistral and failing miserably. It was so big. Thinking about it now, I'm glad I didn't make it. But I saw Cribbar working perfectly, five or six years ago, breaking right round the Point and into Little Fistral, so as far as I know, the good days weren't confined to the sixties. Some days have been ten or fifteen feet and just perfect in the winter~time.

Up and riding.
Aussie Pete Russell takes the first wall, a medium sized right, to get the feel of the session's power and intensity.

One bright but forbidding day in September 1966 was captured on slide by Doug. He drove out to the Head along with scores of others, as some of the largest rideable waves Newquay had ever seen, pumped in with the rising tide. Jack, Aussie Johnny McIlroy and Sydney surfer Pete Russell paddled out mid~morning to challenge the insane walls of deep blue power which had begun pounding Cornwall's North Coast the previous night.

"It was an incredible sight", said Doug, "Cribbar was really working. There were rights and lefts on the wave. The small crew who were out sat and watched for a while as these monsters charged in. Then one by one they took off".

No takers.
Looking more like the North Shore than the North Coast, another right~hand barrel destroys itself on Towan Head.

Brothers in arms.
Jack Lydgate (left) and Johnny McIlroy take the same twelve foot set early on in the session to get used to the speed of Cribbar.

Paddling hard and deep, each clawed his way into the shallow faced 15 foot lumps, before taking a drop that came direct from their own nightmares. Sixty feet further in, the wave disembowled itself on the reef, turning inside out and sucking anything in the way into a foam ball that spectators put at "the size of an average semi".

"Some of the waves were actually bigger than 20 feet. You look at the wave, you measure the surfer and as Jack was six feet tall, some of these brutes were three times overhead. What do you call that? The most remarkable thing was watching Pete, Jack and Johnny paddle back out after making the shoulder. You could see

them sprint~paddling for the top of the wave from the trough, rising up the face with their hand holes of white water pocking the surface and just clipping the pitching lip which must have been two or three feet thick", said Doug.

"It's hard to estimate the exact size ~ but when Jack Lydgate paddled up one wave, he left three hand~hole paddle marks in the face ~ and he wasn't even at the top. He was riding an eleven foot board", said John.

Taken from a dangerous spot, lower down in the rocky gullies below Towan Head, the first of a four wave set feathers almost half a mile out.

Roger Mansfield ~ who last paddled out to look at Cribbar in 1988 when it was breaking at twelve feet ~ was among the crowd who went out to Towan Head. "It was a big, bright but misty day. Word had gone around that some guys were going to try and ride Cribbar. Walking out to the headland, the Bay was closed out and as we came out along Towan Head, the wave which we call the Mystic ~ which is off by Dane Rock and only works when the swell is massive ~ was breaking at ten feet. Three surfers were out trying to ride it"

Chris Jones was one of those surfers. "The Bay was closing out from the Dane rock to Porth Island when The Chin, Robin Wilson and me went out. Mystic Rock was just monstrous. It got it's name because sometimes it's there and sometimes it isn't, it's mysterious. I paddled into one and down in the trough, I could actually see the old Mystic in shallow water in front of me. There it was, that big old solid lump, which few have ever seen, staring back at me".

Rolling thunder.
Another huge set roars in. People on
Towan Head felt the ground shake as
these monsters made landfall.
September 1966.

Roger Mansfield: "There were lines stacked up to the horizon and to this day, it's the biggest surf I have ever been close to in my life. The men went down the lifeboat slipway and paddled out wide around the headland, then came into the swell. Jack got cleaned up, I looked for him for a while. His board got washed up in a big gully in the headland ~ I rescued both halves of it.

"Two rides stand out. Pete Russell was way out in the main peak, waiting. Jack had been cleaned up paddling out even though he had turned turtle in an eskimo roll. He was strong and powerful and managed to swim back round the headland. It would have been impossible to get in at Little Fistral, it was 15 feet. It was a long time before we saw him again.

"Johnny took off on a wave that was relatively inside. It was a left and it really walled up. He dropped in when it wasn't so steep, but he bottom turned and it stooded up hard as it was very close in. Johnny used his last bit of speed to climb the face and throw himself over the lip. He made it, the board didn't. There were no leg ropes then. Johnny managed to swim away into deeper water and his board bounced past into the mass of whitewater and further across to the flat seas on the other side of the headland. It was an epic performance.

"Most notable, though, was the wave by Pete Russell. He was half way down the wave before I realised this giant was being ridden. I heard others shouting 'Wait...look...it is!' and there was a white scar snaking down the left wave face, with a bigger twist in it as Pete turned on the way down. It was so far out, it was so big, the whitewater was rolling slowly. It seemed everything was in slow motion.

Sumpter picks off a right at Fistral's North end, the day after the massive swell. It's still double overhead.

"The wave turned into an enormous shoulder, I'd put it as at least 20 feet. Pete completed the ride by giving it a drawn out bottom turn, which gave him a chance to turn up, fade down a little further and then come off", said Roger.

"Rick Friar, Chris Jones and an unknown South African were out trying to surf the Mystic rock and later that day Rod Sumpter and Bob Head paddled out to challenge this beast of a wave. Sumpter dropped into one set which was three times overhead", said John Conway.

Eventually, all four surfers who were the focus of this memorable day were washed in after taking a pounding from several heart~stopping wipe~outs. Jack came in on the other side of Towan Head. Pete and Johnny were thought to have caught the best waves and had ridden them longest. But Jack had taken on some truly awesome close~outs which had won him lasting respect.

Counting the cost.
A damaged board which is washed
in around the Head and recovered
by local surfers acting as a water
team back~up.

Bale or go?
Aussie Johnny McIlroy gets ready for the inside jack~up,
Cribbar left, September 1966. Johnny still has another six feet of
face to slide in to. Given that this wave is already three times
overhead, how big would you call it?

Raw Atlantic power explodes on cliffs beneath Baker's Folly, Pentire Head. September 1966.

The following day, the swell dropped slightly ~ but Pete Russell was out again, surfing a rare and big right hander at Little Fistral which John Conway put at 12 feet. Peter lost his board and was lucky to get it back in one piece.

"Pete was an amazing surfer", said John. "I travelled to France with him when I was 17. My introduction to Guethary was a rainy morning at 15 feet. Pete paddled out with me and said 'don't worry about it, you just get one wave under your belt and you'll be OK'. It was an education...but he was right, it was really good. I've ridden big waves at Fistral on a long board, when you can sit out the back and get into them early, then kick off if it gets too gnarly. These days, on a shortboard, you take off in the impact zone, it can be much hairier.

Clean~up!
This set caught Johnny, Jack and Pete as they paddled back out. Look at the flawless left, walling up behind the inside dumper.

There would be other big days at Cribbar, but few would be around to try and ride them. This day was a stand~out for a bizarre, unique wave.

It wasn't all blood~and~guts bravado ~ even Iron Men have their weaknesses. Jack Lydgate surfed Cribbar for an hour on his own in the late autumn of 1966 and got wiped out by the second wave of a set. It was big but not critical.

Jack went one way in the inside washing machine, while his board went the other. It washed around into the deep, rocky gullies on the south side of the Head, before it got smashed in pieces. The surfer swam right around Towan Head in the heavy swells and clambered out at the old lifeboat slipway.

Two months later, Cribbar worked for three hours for a short session for this unknown rider.
Looking more like Sunset Beach, the offshore soon switched round to blow it out.

A rare wave opposite the Fly Cellars during the big swell of September 1966

Doug Wilson: "As Jack staggered up the slip, there was a little ice~cream van run by Pip Staffieri, a real character who used to love parking his van near a good break to watch the surfing. He ambled up to Pip, having just come through hell and said 'How about a free ice cream, Pip, for all the trade I've bought you this morning?' Pip, with a big smile, leaned out of his van and handed Jack the biggest ice cream you've ever seen".

These were the surfers who shaped the destiny of British surfing. They defined the best of the sport in the 1990's in our cold, green, northern islands. They passed that mercurial, joyous thrill to each of us as surely as they may have handed us a shared block of wax for an early morning session on those beaches so long ago. It's up to us to keep the faith.

What would it take to make you paddle out?
Money. Fame. Or a priceless personal memory to last you a lifetime?

TEXT

Rod Holmes

PHOTOS

Doug Wilson

DESIGN & REPRO

Scantec

Unit 5a Falmouth Business Park   Falmouth   Cornwall TR11 4SZ

TEL 0326 312619

PRINTING

Linard & Co Web Ltd

11 Holmfield Lane   Thornes   Wakefield   WF2 7AD

TEL 0924 290472

You should have been here yesterday:

A History of British Surfing

first published 1994

ISBN   0 952187 90 6

All rights reserved. No part of this work may be

reproduced by any means without prior

consent of the authors.

© SeasEdge Publications